Bariatric Air Fryer

Quick and Easy Recipes to Prepare
after Surgery and Stay Healthy

Jasmine Cooper

Furthermore, the transmission, duplication, or reproduction of any of the following work including specific information will be considered an illegal act irrespective of if it is done electronically or in print. This extends to creating a secondary or tertiary copy of the work or a recorded copy and is only allowed with the express written consent from the Publisher. All additional right reserved.

The information in the following pages is broadly considered a truthful and accurate account of facts and as such, any inattention, use, or misuse of the information in question by the reader will render any resulting actions solely under their purview. There are no scenarios in which the publisher or the original author of this work can be in any fashion deemed liable for any hardship or damages that may befall them after undertaking information described herein.

Additionally, the information in the following pages is intended only for informational purposes and should thus be thought of as universal. As befitting its nature, it is presented without assurance regarding its prolonged validity or interim quality. Trademarks that are mentioned are done without written consent and can in no way be considered an endorsement from the trademark holder.

Table of Contents

Introduction

Keeping a healthy weight enhances the general quality of our lives, allowing us to perform our daily tasks with ease and comfort.

A healthy weight is good for both our physical and mental well-being.

What starts out as an inappropriate snack, a short, high-carb dinner, or a few extra dishes "to avoid wasting food" can quickly degenerate into a serious health problem. Particularly if we have a genetic inclination to add weight.

Bad food habits can negatively impact our health even before we know what we're doing to the amazing gift of nature that is our bodies. The first and most important obligation we have as human beings is to honor the temple we call home for the rest of our lifetime on this earth.

Health problems related to obesity, such as high cholesterol and blood pressure, type 2 diabetes and obstructive sleep apnea, are all reduced when you lose a sufficient amount of body weight.

Chapter 1: Breakfast Recipes

Breakfast Casserole

Preparation Time: 10 minutes

Cooking Time: 28 minutes

Servings: 4

Ingredients:

- 2 eggs
- 4 egg whites
- 4 tsp pine nuts, minced
- 2/3 cup chicken broth
- 1 lb. beef
- 1/4 cup roasted red pepper, sliced
- 1/4 cup pesto sauce
- 1/8 tsp pepper
- 1/4 tsp sea salt

Directions:

1. Preheat the air fryer to 370°F. Spray air fryer pan with cooking spray and set aside.

2. Heat another pan over medium heat. Add beef to a pan and cook until golden brown.
3. Once cooked then drain excess oil and spread it into the prepared pan.
4. Whisk remaining ingredients except pine nuts in a bowl and pour over beef.
5. Place pan in the air fryer and cook for 25-28 minutes.
6. Top with pine nuts and serve.

Nutrition:

- Calories: 225
- Fat: 49 g
- Carbohydrates: 2 g
- Protein: 39 g

Spinach muffins

Preparation Time: 10 minutes

Cooking Time: 20 minutes

Servings: 8

Ingredients:

- 4 eggs
- 1/2 tsp baking powder
- 1 zucchini, grated
- 1/2 cup feta cheese, crumbled
- 4 onion spring, chopped
- 1/3 cup flour
- 1/4 cup margarine
- 4 tbsp parsley, chopped
- 1/2 tsp nutmeg
- 1/4 cup water
- 1/2 cup spinach, cooked
- 1/4 tsp pepper
- 1/4 tsp salt

Directions:

1. Heat the air fryer to 370°F and whisk together eggs, water, margarine, and salt in a bowl. Add baking powder and flour and mix well After add onions, nutmeg, parsley, spinach, zucchini and mix well.

2. Add feta cheese and mix well. Season with pepper and salt.

3. Pour batter into the silicone muffin molds and put in the air fryer. Cook for 20 minutes.

4. Serve and enjoy.

Nutrition:

- Calories: 135
- Fat: 18.1 g
- Carbohydrates: 4.2 g
- Protein: 56 g

Broccoli Muffins

Preparation Time: 10 minutes

Cooking Time: 24 minutes

Servings: 6

Ingredients:

- 2 large eggs
- 1 cup broccoli florets, chopped
- 1 cup unsweetened almond milk
- 2 cups almond flour
- 1 tsp baking powder
- 2 tbsp nutritional yeast
- 1/2 tsp sea salt

Directions:

1. Preheat the air fryer to 325°F.
2. Add all ingredients into the large bowl and mix until well combined.
3. Pour mixture into the silicone muffin molds and place into the air fryer basket.
4. Cook muffins for 20-24 minutes.
5. Serve and enjoy.

Nutrition:

- Calories: 160
- Fat: 21.2 g
- Carbohydrates: 11 g

- Protein: 32 g

Zucchini Gratin

Preparation Time: 10 minutes

Cooking Time: 24 minutes

Servings: 4

Ingredients:

- 1 large egg, lightly beaten
- 1 1/4 cup unsweetened almond milk
- 3 medium zucchinis, sliced
- 1 tbsp Dijon mustard
- 1/2 cup nutritional yeast
- 1 tsp sea salt

Directions:

1. Preheat the air fryer to 370°F.
2. Arrange zucchini slices in the air fryer baking dish.
3. In a saucepan, heat almond milk over low heat and stir in Dijon mustard, nutritional yeast, and sea salt. Add beaten egg and whisk well.
4. Pour sauce over zucchini slices.
5. Place dish in the air fryer and cook for 20-24 minutes.
6. Serve and enjoy.

Nutrition:

- Calories: 120
- Fat: 3.4 g

- Carbohydrates: 8 g
- Protein: 33 g

Pepper Egg Bites

Preparation Time: 15 minutes
Cooking Time: 15 minutes
Servings: 7
Ingredients:

- 5 large eggs, beaten
- 3 tablespoons 2% milk
- 1/2 teaspoon dried marjoram
- 1/8 teaspoon salt
- Pinch freshly ground black pepper
- 1/3 cup minced bell pepper, any color
- 3 tablespoons minced scallions
- 1/2 cup shredded Colby or Muenster cheese

Directions:

1. In a medium bowl, combine the eggs, milk, salt, marjoram and black pepper. mix until well combined.

2. Stir peppers, scallions, and cheese; fill the 7 egg bite cups with the egg mixture. You must sure some of the solids in each cup. Heat the air fryer to 325°F.

3. Make a foil sling and fold an 18-inch-long piece of heavy-duty aluminum foil lengthwise into thirds. Place the egg bite pan on this sling and lower it into the air fryer.

4. Leave the foil in the air fryer, but bend down the edges to make fit in the appliance.

5. Bake the egg bites for 10 to 15 minutes.

6. Remove the egg bite pan with the foil sling. Let cool for 5 minutes, then invert the pan onto a plate and serve warm.

Nutrition:
- Calories: 87
- Total fat: 6 g
- Carbohydrates: 1 g
- Protein: 42 g

Chapter 2: Snacks Recipes

Vegetarian Toast

Preparation Time: 12 minutes

Cooking Time: 13 minutes

Servings: 4

Ingredients:

- 1 red bell pepper, cut into 1/2-inch strips
- 1 cup sliced button or cremini mushrooms
- 1 small yellow squash, sliced
- 2 green onions, cut into 1/2-inch slices
- Extra light olive oil for misting
- 4 to 6 pieces sliced Italian or French bread
- 2 tablespoons softened butter
- 1/2 cup soft goat cheese

Directions:

1. Combine the mushrooms, red pepper, green onions and squash in the air fryer and mist with oil. Roast for 9 minutes or until the vegetables are tender. Shake the basket once during cooking time.

2. Remove the vegetables from the basket and set aside.
3. Spread the bread with butter and place butter-side up in the air fryer. Toast until golden brown, for about 4 minutes.
4. Spread the goat cheese on the toasted bread, and top with the vegetables.

Nutrition:

- Calories: 162
- Total Fat: 11 g
- Carbohydrates: 9 g
- Protein: 37 g

Chimichanga

Preparation Time: 2 minutes

Cooking Time: 5/8 minutes

Servings: 1

Ingredients:

- 1 whole-grain tortilla
- 1/2 cup vegan refried beans
- 1/4 cup grated vegan cheese (optional)
- Cooking oil spray (sunflower, safflower)
- 1/2 cup fresh salsa
- 2 cups chopped romaine lettuce (about 1/2 head)
- Guacamole (optional)
- Chopped cilantro (optional)
- Cheesy Sauce (optional)

Directions:

1. Lay the tortilla on a flat surface and put the beans in the center. Top with the cheese, if you want.

2. Wrap the bottom up over the filling, and then fold in the sides. Then roll it all up to enclose the beans inside the tortilla.

3. Spray the air fryer basket with oil, put the tortilla wrap inside the basket, seam-side down. Spray the top of the chimichanga with oil.

4. Fry for about 5/8 minutes at 350F and spray the top and sides with oil; flip over and spray the other side with oil. Fry until browned and crisp.
5. Transfer to a plate and top with the salsa, guacamole, lettuce, cilantro, and Cheesy Sauce, if you want. Serve immediately.

Nutrition:

- Calories: 187
- Total fat: 6 g
- Carbohydrates: 25 g
- Protein: 53 g

Tacos Crispy Avocado

Preparation Time: 10 minutes

Cooking Time: 10 minutes

Servings: 5

Ingredients:

Salsa:

- 1 garlic clove minced
- 1 Roma tomato, finely chopped
- 1 cup finely chopped pineapple
- 1/2 red bell pepper, finely chopped
- 1/2 of a medium red onion
- Pinch each cumin and salt
- ½ not spicy jalapeno finely chopped

Avocado tacos:

- 1 avocado
- 1/2 cup panko crumbs (65 g)
- 1 large egg whisked
- 1/4 cup all-purpose flour (35 g)
- 4 flour tortillas
- Pinch each salt and pepper

Adobo Sauce:

- 1/4 tsp lime juice
- 1/4 cup plain yogurt (60 g)

- 1 tbsp. Adobo sauce from a jar of chipotle peppers
- 2 tbsp. Mayonnaise (30 g)
- Polte peppers

Directions:

1. Sauce: mix all sauce ingredients together and refrigerate.

2. Prepare avocado: halve the length of the avocado, remove the stone and place the avocado skin face down; cut each half into 4 equal pieces. Then gently peel off the skin.

3. Prep station: heat t air fryer to 190°C. Arrange your work area so you have a bowl of flour, a bowl of whisk, a bowl of Panko with S & P, and a baking sheet lined with baking paper at the end.

4. Coating: dip each avocado slice in flour, egg, and then panko. Place on the prepared baking sheet and fry in the air fryer for 10 minutes at 190°C.

5. Sauce: While cooking avocados, mix all sauce ingredients together.

6. Serving: Place salsa on a tortilla and add 2 pieces of avocado. Drizzle with salsa and serve immediately.

Nutrition:

- Calories: 93
- Protein: 53.7 g
- Fat: 13.25 g
- Carbohydrates: 4.69 g

Apple chips with cinnamon and yogurt sauce

Preparation Time: 5 minutes

Cooking Time: 12 minutes

Servings: 4

Ingredients:

- 230 g apple (such as Fuji or Honeycrisp)
- 1 tsp. ground cinnamon
- 2 tsp. canola oil
- Cooking oil spray (as needed)
- 1/4 cup plain 1% low-fat Greek yogurt
- 1 tsp. honey
- 1 tbsp. almond butter

Directions:

1. Heat the fryer unit to reach 375°Fahrenheit/191°Celsius.

2. Thinly slice the apple on a mandoline. Toss the slices in a bowl with cinnamon and canola oil to evenly cover.

3. Spritz the fryer basket using cooking spray.

4. Arrange seven to eight sliced apples in the basket (single-layered).

5. Air-fry them for 12 minutes at 375° F (flipping them every 4 min.), and rearranging slices to

flatten them. They will continue to crisp upon cooling. Continue the procedure with the rest of the apple slices.

6.   Whisk the yogurt with the almond butter and honey in a mixing container until smooth.

7.   Arrange six to eight sliced apples on each plate with a small dollop of dipping sauce.

Nutrition:

- Carbohydrates: 17 g
- Fat: 3 g
- Protein: 58 g
- Calories: 104

Mozzarella Cheese Bites with Marinara Sauce

Preparation Time: 15 minutes
Cooking Time: 1 hour + 6/10 minutes
Servings: 12 cheese bites or 6 servings
Ingredients:

- 1 egg, lightly beaten
- 1 tbsp. water
- 1/2 cup all-purpose flour
- 1/2 tbsp. salt
- 1/2 tsp. dried Italian seasoning
- 3/4 cup panko breadcrumbs
- 6 Mozzarella cheese sticks
- Cooking spray
- 3/4 cup marinara sauce
- Red Pepper, to taste (very little)

Directions:

1. Slice the mozzarella cheese sticks in half—crosswise.
2. Whisk egg with water in a shallow mixing dish.
3. Stir the flour with the salt and Italian seasoning in another shallow dish.
4. Place breadcrumbs in a third shallow dish.
5. Dip the cheese sticks into the egg mixture, then cover using the flour mixture. Dredge again into the egg mix, then into breadcrumbs until coated.

6. Arrange them on a baking tray—freeze until firm (1 hr.).
7. Preheat the Air Fryer to reach 360°Fahrenheit/182°Celsius.
8. Lightly coat the fryer basket using a spritz of cooking spray.
9. Place frozen cheese bites in the Air Fryer (single-layered), working in batches if necessary, being careful not to crowd.
10. Cook in the preheated air fryer until golden brown and cheese just begins to melt (4-6 min.). Repeat with the rest of the bites.
11. Meanwhile, whisk the marinara sauce and red pepper to your liking.
12. Serve the bites with marinara sauce.

Nutrition:
- Carbohydrates: 22.6 g
- Fat: Content: 6.7 g
- Protein: 50.9 g
- Calories: 122.9

Chapter 3: Appetizer Recipes

Easy Air Fryer Biscuits

Preparation Time: 5 minutes

Cooking Time: 6/10 minutes

Servings: 4

Ingredients:

- 2 tbsp butter, melted
- 1 cup shredded cheddar cheese
- 2 large eggs
- 1/2 tsp baking powder
- 1 cup almond flour
- 1/4 tsp pink Himalayan salt
- 2 tbsp sour cream

Directions:

1. Place the baking powder, almond flour, and salt in a big container.
2. Mix the cheddar cheese by hand until well combined.

3. Add the eggs, butter, and sour cream to the center and mix with a large fork, spoon, or your hands, until a sticky dough form.
4. Place a piece of parchment paper in your deep fryer basket. Drop 1/4 cup (for large) or 2 tablespoons (for small) portions of dough onto parchment.
5. Air Fry/"Bake" at 400°F for 6 minutes (for small ones) to 10 minutes (for large ones), until golden brown and cooked through. Repeat with the remaining batter as needed.
6. Serve immediately!

Nutrition:

- Calories: 117
- Fat: 15 g
- Carbohydrates: 3 g
- Protein: 47 g

Crispy Potatoes

Preparation Time: 10 minutes

Cooking Time: 18/20 minutes

Servings: 6

Ingredients:

- 3/4 teaspoon kosher salt
- 1/4 teaspoon coarse ground black pepper, more to taste
- 1 tablespoon olive oil or avocado oil
- 1-pound potatoes, cut into 1/2-inch chunks
- Seasoning mixture, if desired

Directions:

1. Heat the fryer to 400°F.
2. In a large bowl, combine the potatoes, oil, salt, and pepper.
3. If desired, add seasoning mix;
4. Stir well.
5. Place in the fryer and cook 18-20 minutes or until tender and golden with a fork, stirring at least once to cook evenly.

Nutrition:

- Calories: 122
- Fat: 9 g
- Carbohydrates: 32 g

- Protein: 44 g

Healthy Cheeseburger Bites

Preparation Time: 10 minutes

Cooking Time: 23/25 minutes

Servings: 4

Ingredients:

- 1/2 cup Shredded Parmesan
- 1/4 cup Reduced Sugar Ketchup
- 1 lb. Lean Ground Beef
- 3 tbsp Mustard
- 1/2 cup Breadcrumbs
- 50 g Dill Pickles, finely diced
- 1/2 cup Fat: -Free Shredded Cheddar
- 3/4 cup Liquid Egg Whites

Directions:

1. Preheat oven to 400°F and spray 24 muffin pan with nonstick cooking spray.
2. Brown ground beef (or meat of your choice) in a large skillet over medium-high heat.
3. While the meat is cooking, mix the remaining ingredients in a large bowl.
4. After cooling briefly, add the cooked meat to the remaining ingredients, stirring until smooth.

5. Pour batter into mini muffin pan, making sure to remove any excess between the slots.
6. Bake 23-25 minutes to 400°F or until muffin tops are golden brown.

Nutrition:

- Calories: 48
- Fat: 1.3 g
- Carbohydrates: 2.3 g
- Protein: 76.8 g

Vegan Sausage, Egg and Cheese Bites

Preparation Time: 10 minutes

Cooking Time: 20/25 minutes

Servings: 6

Ingredients:

- 1 lb. vegan sausage, cooked and slightly cooled
- 4 ounces cream cheese, softened
- 1 cup shredded cheddar
- 1/3 cup coconut flour
- 1/2 teaspoon baking powder
- 3 eggs, beaten

Directions:

1. Preheat the air fryer to 350°F.
2. Cook vegan sausage for breakfast, drained and set aside to slightly cool.
3. After the vegan sausage has cooled, add it to a bowl and combine with the cream cheese until no lumps of cream cheese remain.
4. Stir in the cheese, eggs, coconut flour and baking powder.
5. Once the mixture is well incorporated, let it cool for 5-10 minutes. The coconut flour continues to absorb moisture, so if it looks runny, it won't be.

6. Oil a cookie sheet and, by using a small kitchen spoon, arrange the egg and cheese sausages on the baking sheet.
7. Bake in air fryer for 18 to 20 minutes to 350°F.
8. Serve and enjoy!

Nutrition:

- Calories: 79
- Fat: 5.9 g
- Carbohydrates: 1.2 g
- Protein: 65 g

Edamame and Garlic

Preparation Time: 5 minutes
Cooking Time: 9 minutes
Servings: 4
Ingredients:

- 1 bag frozen edamame in pods
- 2 tablespoon olive oil, divided
- 1/2 teaspoon garlic salt
- 1/2 teaspoon salt
- 1/4 teaspoon freshly ground black pepper

Directions:

1. In a medium bowl put the edamame and drizzle with 1 tablespoon of olive oil.
2. Mix to coat well.
3. In a small bowl stir the garlic salt, pepper, salt.
4. Pour the mixture into the bowl of edamame and mix until the edamame is fully coated.
5. Pour in your air fryer basket the rest of the 1 tablespoon of olive oil.
6. Put the edamame in the greased basket.
7. Set temperature of your Air Fryer to 375°F and cook for 9 minutes.
8. Stir the edamame once halfway through the cooking time.

Nutrition:

- Calories: 170

- Carbohydrates: 26 g
- Fat: 7 g
- Protein: 41 g

Chapter 4: Chicken and Poultry Recipes

Chicken wings with cheese and yogurt sauce

Preparation Time: 15 minutes

Cooking Time: 29/30 minutes

Servings: 6

Ingredients:

For the Chicken Wings:

- 2 tbsp. baking powder
- 2 lbs. chicken wings
- 2 tbsp. Seasoning Blend
- Olive oil or coconut oil spray

For the wing sauce:

- 3/4 cup favorite not spicy Sauce
- 1/2 tbsp. grass-fed butter

For the Yogurt Cheese Sauce:

- 1/4 cup buttermilk
- 1 tbsp apple cider vinegar
- 2 oz crumbled blue cheese

- 8 oz container of non-fat Icelandic Yogurt
- 1/3 tsp salt

Directions:

For the Chicken Wings:

1. Pat the chicken wings dry by using paper towels.
2. In a large bowl, add Dry Seasoning Mix and baking powder until lightly coated. If desired, you can place the chicken wings in a large paper bag or large Ziplock bag to evenly coat
3. Preheat the fryer basket to 390°F for about 1-2 minutes to prevent sticking
4. Spray wings lightly with cooking spray
5. Put the wings in the basket in one layer, do not stack them on top of each other
6. Cook for 4 minutes at 390°F, then stir and turn with tongs
7. Cook for an additional 3 minutes at 390°F, spray again lightly with cooking spray and flip again
8. Cook again for 4 minutes at 390°F
9. Check and flip if needed, cook for an additional 9 minutes at 360°F, then flip and stir again.
10. Cook for the last 9 minutes at 360°F

11. In a huge container, pitch the chicken wings with Sauce and butter.

For the Yogurt Dipping Sauce:

1. In a medium-size bowl, mix buttermilk, yogurt, salt, apple cider vinegar, and blue cheese.
2. Serving size is 2 tbsp.
   Serve the chicken wings with a little sauce next to them.

Nutrition:

- Carbohydrates: 1 g
- Fat: 1.7 g
- Protein: 43 g
- Calories: 113

Low-Carbohydrates Chicken Burger

Preparation Time: 10 minutes

Cooking Time: 20 minutes

Servings: 3

Ingredients:

- 1 oz Low-Moisture Part-Skim Mozzarella Cheese Shredded
- 1/4 cup Green Onions Chopped
- 1 pound Ground Chicken
- 1/4 cup Mayonnaise

Directions:

1. Shredded chicken (you can use a food processor for this if you prefer)
2. Chop the green onions and mix them with the chicken mixture.
3. Add Mayo and Mozzarella Cheese, mix well
4. Form four equal patties
5. Cook in the air fryer at 320°for 10 minutes on each side

Nutrition:

- Calories: 135
- Fat: 14 g
- Carbohydrate: 4 g

- Protein: 34 g

Air Fryer Chicken Breast

Preparation Time: 10 minutes

Cooking Time: 10/15 minutes

Servings: 4

Ingredients:

- 1/2 teaspoon salt
- 1/4 teaspoon pepper
- 4 boneless chicken breasts
- 1/4 teaspoon garlic powder
- 2 tablespoons butter

Directions:

1. Place the boneless chicken breasts on a cutting board.
2. Melt the butter in the microwave and add garlic powder, salt, and pepper. Mix to combine.
3. Coat the chicken with the butter mixture on both sides.
4. Place the chicken in the fryer in a single layer.
5. Cook the chicken at 380°for 10-15 minutes, flipping it in half.
6. Let the chicken rest for 5 minutes.
7. Serve immediately.

Nutrition:

- Calories: 120

- Fat: 6 g
- Carbohydrates: 0 g
- Protein: 37 g

Low Carbohydrates Fried Chicken Recipe

Preparation Time: 10 minutes

Cooking Time: 15-30 minutes

Servings: 4

Ingredients:

- 1/4 tsp freshly ground black pepper
- 25 g/1/4 cup coconut flour
- 55 g/1 cup crushed pork rinds/pork scratching
- 1/2 tsp garlic powder (optional)
- 1/2 tsp salt
- 2 large eggs
- 1 lb. chicken tenders

Directions:

1. Combine coconut flour with the salt and pepper in a medium bowl and mix until consistent.
2. Whisk the eggs in a second bowl.
3. Combine minced pork rinds/pork rinds in the third bowl with garlic powder, if using.
4. Dredge each piece in the flour mixture, dip it into the egg, shake off the excess, and then lightly press into the pork rind mixture to coat all sides.
5. Reserve until you are ready to cook.

6. Preheat the fryer to 200°C/400°F for 5 minutes. Place the coated chicken in the fryer basket in a single layer and cook for about 15-30 minutes at 400°F until fully cooked and crisp.

7. Cook in batches if necessary and keep those that were cooked first warm in a low oven or under foil.

8. Serve immediately with your choice of sides, or chill, then serve as part of a lunch box if desired.

Nutrition:

- Calories: 206
- Protein: 49.3 g
- Carbohydrate: 1.5 g
- Fat: 10.7 g

Chicken Parmesan

Preparation Time: 5 minutes
Cooking Time: 6/15 minutes
Servings: 2
Ingredients:

- 6 tbsp seasoned breadcrumbs
- 1/2 cup marinara
- 1 tbsp butter, melted (or olive oil)
- 2 tbsp grated Parmesan cheese
- Cooking spray
- 2 (8 oz) each chicken breast, sliced in half
- 6 tbsp reduced-fat mozzarella cheese

Directions:

1. Preheat the fryer to 360°F for 3 minutes.
2. Combine the breadcrumbs and Parmesan cheese in a bowl. Melt the butter in another bowl.
3. Lightly butter the chicken, then dip it into the breadcrumb mixture.
4. When the fryer is ready, place 2 pieces in the basket and spray the top with oil.
5. Cook 6 minutes to 360°F, turn and top each with 2 tablespoons sauce and 1 ½ tablespoon grated mozzarella cheese.
6. Cook until cheese is melted.
7. Reserve and keep warm, repeat with the remaining 2 pieces.

Nutrition:

- Protein: 31.5 g
- Fat: 9.5 g
- Cholesterol: 14mg
- Fiber: 1.5 g
- Carbo: 12 g

Chapter 5: Meat Recipes

Air Fryer Steak Bites and Mushrooms

Preparation Time: 5 minutes

Cooking Time: 20 minutes

Servings: 2

Ingredients:

- 1 tsp Worcestershire sauce (not spicy)
- 8 oz sliced mushrooms
- 1/2 tsp minced garlic dried
- 1/4 tsp pepper
- 1 lb. lean sirloin steak diced into cubes
- Spray butter, to taste
- Salt to taste (very little)

Directions:

1. Peel and dice the steak into 1-inch cubes.
2. Preheat the Air Fryer to 400°F for 4 minutes.
3. Add sliced mushrooms to the steak.

4. Spray butter spray three times, mix. Spray three more times, mix. Add Worcestershire, 1/2 teaspoon dried minced garlic, and 1/4 teaspoon pepper, mix.
5. Spread the mixture on the bottom of the fryer.
6. Fry in the air at 400°F for 12 minutes, stirring the mixture halfway through cooking.
7. Add more time if you prefer the steak to be more cooked, 3 to 5 minutes longer.
8. Season to taste and serve.

Nutrition:

- Calories: 168
- Carbohydrates: 2 g
- Protein: 57 g
- Fat: 5 g

Meatball Casserole

Preparation Time: 15 minutes

Cooking Time: 15/18 minutes

Servings: 6

Ingredients:

- 1 tbsp. Thyme, chopped
- 0.25 cup Parsley, chopped
- 0.33 lb. Turkey sausage
- 1 Egg, beaten
- 0.66 lb. Ground beef
- 2 tbsp. Olive oil
- 1 Shallot, minced
- 1 tbsp. Dijon mustard
- 3 Garlic cloves, minced
- 2 tbsp. Skimmed milk
- 1 tbsp. Rosemary, chopped
- 1 cup Bread crumbs

Directions:

1. Preheat the air fryer to 400°F by placing a little oil in the basket.
2. Add shallots, garlic and cook for 3 minutes at 400°F to soften.
3. In a bowl add and mix the milk and breadcrumbs; then add the rosemary, mustard, ground beef, egg,

turkey sausage, chopped parsley, thyme and set aside to macerate.

4. After five minutes use this mixture to make small patties and add them to the fryer.
5. Cook the meatballs at 400°F for 15 minutes, about halfway through cooking open and flip the meatballs so they are evenly cooked on all sides.

Nutrition:

- Calories: 168
- Carbohydrates: 4 g
- Protein: 52 g
- Fat: 11 g

Baked Beef

Preparation Time: 1 hour

Cooking Time: 1 hour

Servings: 3

Ingredients:

- 1 bunch garlic cloves
- 1 bunch fresh herbs, mixed
- 2 onions, sliced
- 1 tbsp. olive oil
- 3 lbs. beef
- 2 celery sticks, chopped
- 2 carrots, chopped

Directions:

1. Heat up a pan and then add the herbs, olive oil, beef roast, and vegetables inside.
2. Turn the air fryer on to 400° and place the pan inside. Let this heat up and close the lid.
3. After 1 hour of cooking, open the lid and then serve this right away.

Nutrition:

- Calories: 206
- Carbohydrates: 10 g
- Fat: 21 g
- Protein: 62 g

Quick and Easy Rib-Eye Steak

Preparation Time: 40 minutes

Cooking Time: 14/18 minutes

Servings: 2

Ingredients:

- 2 lb. Unchilled steak
- 1 tbsp. Olive oil
- Steak Rub: Salt and pepper mix (desired, very little)
- Baking pan also needed to fit into the basket

Directions:

1. Press the "M" button for the French Fries icon. Adjust the time to 4 minutes at 400°Fahrenheit.
2. Rub the steak with the oil and seasonings.
3. Arrange the steak in the basket and air-fry for 14/18 minutes. (Flip it over after 7/9 minutes.)
4. Place the rib-eye on a platter, and let it rest for ten minutes.
5. Slice it and garnish the way you like it.

Nutrition:

- Calories: 260
- Protein: 129.44 g
- Fat: 55.78 g

- Carbohydrates: 0 g

Roast Beef

Preparation Time: 1 hour
Cooking Time: 55 minutes
Servings: 6
Ingredients:

- 1/2 tsp. Garlic powder
- 1/2 tsp. Oregano
- 1 tsp. Dried thyme
- 1 tbsp. Olive oil
- 2 lb. Round roast

Directions:

1. Heat the Air Fryer at 330°Fahrenheit.
2. Combine the spices.
3. Brush the oil over the beef, and rub it using the spice mixture.
4. Add to a baking dish and arrange it in the Air Fryer basket for 30 minutes to 330°F.
5. Turn it over and continue cooking 25 minutes more.
6. Wait for a few minutes before slicing.
7. Serve on your choice of bread or plain with a delicious side dish.

Nutrition:

- Calories: 187
- Protein: 45.97 g
- Fat: 10.01 g
- Carbohydrates: 0.28 g

Chapter 6: Fish and Seafood Recipes

Healthy Air Fryer Baked Salmon

Preparation Time: 10 minutes

Cooking Time: 15 minutes

Servings: 2

Ingredients:

- 1 teaspoon olive oil
- 2 6-ounce salmon fillets, skinless and boneless
- Black pepper, to taste (very little)
- Kosher salt, to taste (very little)

Directions:

1. Coat the salmon with a little oil. Spice salmon with salt and pepper.
2. Place the salmon in the basket. Air-fry the salmon at 360°F until cooked to your desired texture, approx. 15 minutes.
3. Check the salmon with a fork to make sure it is cooked the way you like it.

4. Enjoy! It is easy.

Nutrition:

- Calories: 159
- Fat: 12 g
- Cholesterol 93 mg
- Protein: 83 g

Crunchy Air Fryer Fish

Preparation Time: 5 minutes

Cooking Time: 10/15 minutes

Servings: 4

Ingredients:

- 1/2 cup yellow cornmeal
- 1/2 tsp garlic powder
- 1 large egg
- 1 tsp coarse salt
- 1/2 tsp black pepper
- 1 lb. white fish fillets
- Lemon and parsley for garnish (Optional)
- Oil spray

Directions:

1. Preheat the air fryer for 3 minutes at 400°F.
2. Beat the egg in a shallow skillet.
3. In a different deep skillet, mix the cornmeal and spices.
4. Dry the fish completely.
5. Drop the fish fillets in the egg; allow extra drip into the pan.
6. Press the fish into the cornmeal combination until well crusted on the two sides.

7. Place the coated fish in the basket of the preheated fryer. Spray lightly with oil.

8. Cook for 10 minutes at 400°F, tossing the fish to ensure uniform cooking.

9. If there are dry spots, spray a little oil. Take back the basket to the air fryer and cook until the fish is well prepared.

10. Lightly squeeze with lemon and sprinkle with parsley.

11. Serve immediately.

Nutrition:

- Calories: 191
- Carbohydrates: 15 g
- Protein: 64 g
- Fat: 3 g

Tuna Zucchini Melts

Preparation Time: 15 minutes

Cooking Time: 7/8 minutes

Servings: 4

Ingredients:

- 4 corn tortillas (unsalted)
- 3 tablespoons softened margarine
- 1 (6-ounce) can chunk light tuna, drained
- 1 cup shredded zucchini, drained by squeezing in a kitchen towel
- 1/3 cup mayonnaise
- 2 tablespoons mustard
- 1 cup parmesan cheese

Directions:

1. Coat tortillas with softened margarine.
2. Put in the basket of the air fryer and grill for 2 to 3 minutes at 350°F or until the tortillas are crispy
3. Take out of basket and set aside.
4. Combine the tuna, zucchini, mayonnaise and mustard in a medium bowl and mix well.
5. Split the tuna mixture between the toasted tortillas. Fold the tortillas together and top each tortilla with a little cheese.

6. Grill for 2-4 minutes in the air fryer at 350°F or until tuna mixture is hot and cheese is melted and beginning to brown. Serve.

Nutrition:

- Calories: 228
- Total Fat: 30 g
- Carbohydrates: 19 g
- Protein: 52 g

Buttery Cod

Preparation Time: 5 minutes

Cooking Time: 12/15 minutes

Servings: 4

Ingredients:

- 1 tbsp. Parsley, chopped
- 3 tbsp. Butter, melted
- 8 Cherry tomatoes, halved
- 0.25 cup Tomato sauce
- 2 Cod fillets, cubed

Directions:

1. Turn on the fryer to 390°F and heat for 2-3 minutes.

2. Combine Butter, Cherry tomatoes, Tomato sauce, Parsley and Cod fillets put them into a pan that works with the air fryer.

3. Place the pan in the air fryer and cook for about 12/15 minutes to 390°F.

4. After 12 minutes of cooking, divide into four bowls and enjoy.

Nutrition:

- Calories: 132
- Carbohydrates: 5 g
- Protein: 51 g
- Fat: 8 g

Breaded Coconut Shrimp

Preparation Time: 5 minutes
Cooking Time: 10/15 minutes
Servings: 4
Ingredients:

- 450 g shrimp
- 1 cup panko breadcrumbs
- 1 cup shredded coconut
- 2 eggs
- 1/3 cup all-purpose flour

Directions:

1. Preheat the air fryer to 360°Fahrenheit for 3-4 minutes.
2. Peel and devein the shrimp.
3. Pour the flour into a bowl.
4. In another bowl, beat the eggs, and in a third bowl, combine the breadcrumbs and coconut.
5. Dip the cleaned shrimp into the flour, eggs, and finish with the coconut mixture.
6. Lightly spray the fryer basket and bake for 10-15 minutes to 360°Fahrenheit or until golden brown.

Nutrition:

- Calories: 185
- Fat: 12.8 g
- Carbohydrates: 3.7 g
- Protein: 38.1 g

Chapter 7: Vegetable Recipes

Buffalo Cauliflower Recipe

Preparation Time: 5 minutes

Cooking Time: 12/15 minutes

Servings: 4

Ingredients:

- 1 cup buffalo sauce (not spicy)
- 1 cup ranch seasoning, if desired (not spicy)
- 1 cup blue cheese seasoning, if desired
- 1 whole cauliflower cut into florets
- Cooking Spray

Directions:

1. Preheat the fryer to 360°F. Spray the fryer basket or pan with cooking spray.

2. Add the cauliflower florets to a large bowl. Pour 1/2 of the buffalo sauce into the florets and mix to coat them with sauce. Place cauliflower florets in the prepared skillet and air fry for 12-15 minutes to 360°F, stirring every 5 minutes.

3. Serve with remaining buffalo sauce, ranch dressing and blue cheese dressing, if desired.

Nutrition:

- Calories: 123
- Carbohydrates: 4 g
- Protein: 24 g
- Fat: 11 g

Mozzarella Radish Salad

Preparation Time: 8-10 min

Cooking Time: 3 min

Servings: 4

Ingredients:

- 1 1/2 pounds radishes, trimmed and halved
- 2 tablespoons olive oil
- Pepper and salt, as needed (very little)

For the Salad:

- 1 teaspoon olive oil
- 1 tablespoon balsamic vinegar
- 1/2-pound mozzarella, sliced
- 1 teaspoon honey
- Pepper and salt, as needed (very little)

Directions:

1. In a medium-sized bowl, thoroughly mix and season the radishes, salt, black pepper and oil.

2. Place your air fryer on a flat kitchen surface; plug it and turn it on. Set temperature to 350°F and let it preheat for 4-5 minutes.

3. Add the mixture to the basket. Push the air-frying basket in the air fryer. Cook for 3 minutes.

4. In a medium sized bowl, thoroughly mix the fried radish and mozzarella cheese.

5. In a bowl of small size, thoroughly mix the other ingredients and serve over the salad!

Nutrition:

- Calories: 163
- Fat: 29 g
- Carbohydrates: 4 g
- Protein: 32 g

Delicious Air Fryer Cauliflower

Preparation Time: 5 minutes

Cooking Time: 10 minutes

Servings: 6

Ingredients:

- 1/2 tsp fresh lemon juice
- 3 cups cauliflower
- Salt and pepper to taste (very little)
- 1 tbsp fresh parsley, chopped
- ¾ tsp dried oregano
- 1 1/2 tsp olive oil
- 1 tbsp pine nuts (unsalted)

Directions:

1. Place the cauliflower in a container and sprinkle with olive oil. Add oregano, salt, and pepper.
2. Place in the fryer at 375°F and fry for 10 minutes.
3. Drop into a serving dish and include pine nuts, fresh parsley, and lemon juice.

Nutrition:

- Calories: 104
- Fat: 7 g
- Carbohydrates: 9 g
- Protein: 44 g

Spinach Quiche

Preparation Time: 10 minutes

Cooking Time: 18/22 minutes

Servings: 3

Ingredients:

- 3 eggs
- 1 cup frozen chopped spinach, thawed and drained
- 1/3 cup heavy cream
- 2 tablespoons honey mustard
- 1/2 cup grated Swiss or Havarti cheese
- 1/2 teaspoon dried thyme
- Pinch salt (very little)
- Freshly ground black pepper, to taste (very little)
- Nonstick baking spray with flour

Directions:

1. In a medium bowl, beat the eggs until blended. Add the spinach, cream, honey mustard, cheese, thyme, salt and pepper and mix evenly.
2. Spray a fryer basket or fryer-friendly pan with nonstick spray. Pour the egg mixture inside.
3. Cook for 18-22 minutes in the air fryer at 380°F or until the egg mixture is puffed, lightly golden and set.

4. Let cool for 5 minutes, then cut into wedges to serve.

Nutrition:

- Calories: 203
- Total Fat: 15 g
- Carbohydrates: 6 g
- Protein: 71 g

Yellow Squash Fritters

Preparation Time: 15 minutes
Cooking Time: 7/9 minutes
Servings: 4
Ingredients:

- 1 (3-ounce) package cream cheese, softened
- 1 egg, beaten
- 1/2 teaspoon dried oregano
- Pinch salt (very little)
- Freshly ground black pepper, to taste (very little)
- 1 medium yellow summer squash, grated
- 1/3 cup grated carrot
- 2/3 cup bread crumbs
- 2 tablespoons olive oil

Directions:

1. In a medium bowl, combine and mix well the cream cheese with the egg, oregano, salt and pepper. Add the pumpkin and the carrot and mix well. Add the breadcrumbs and mix well.
2. Form about 2 tablespoons of this mixture into a patty about 1/2 inch thick. Repeat with remaining mixture. Brush pancakes with olive oil.
3. Air-fry until crisp and golden at 380°F, about 7 to 9 minutes.

Nutrition:

- Calories: 134
- Total Fat: 17 g
- Carbohydrates: 16 g
- Protein: 56 g

Chapter 8: Side Dishes Recipes

Baked Ricotta

Preparation Time: 10 minutes

Cooking Time: 20/22 minutes

Servings: 4

Ingredients:

- Pinch of Salt and pepper (very little)
- 1/8 tsp garlic powder
- 15- ounce Part-skim ricotta
- 1/3 cup parmesan cheese
- Olive Oil Spray
- 1/8 tsp basil
- 1 cup of marinara sauce (not spicy)

Directions:

1. Preheat the air fryer to 350°F for 2 minutes.
2. Drizzle 5 ramekins with olive oil and place them on a baking sheet.
3. In a small bowl, add garlic powder, ricotta cheese, basil, salt, Parmesan cheese and pepper.

4. Stir the ricotta mixture to blend completely.
5. Using a spoon, fill the prepared ramekins with the ricotta mixture.
6. On top of each ricotta ramekin true a spoonful of sweet marinara sauce.
7. Bake for 20/22 minutes at 350F.
8. Take out and serve

Nutrition:

- Calories: 144
- Carbohydrates: 5 g
- Protein: 72 g
- Fat: 8 g

Simple Buttered Potatoes

Preparation Time: 5 minutes

Cooking Time: 25 minutes

Servings: 4

Ingredients:

- 1-pound potatoes, cut into wedges
- 2 garlic cloves, grated
- 1 Tsp fennel seeds
- 1 Tbsp unsalted butter, melted
- Salt and black pepper to taste (very little)

Directions:

1. In a bowl, mix the potatoes, butter, garlic, fennel seeds, salt and black pepper until seasoned well.
2. Place the potatoes in the basket of the air fryer.
3. Bake at 360°F for 25 minutes, shaking once during cooking, until crisp on the outside and tender on the inside.
4. Serve.

Nutrition:

- Calories: 100
- Carbohydrates: 8 g
- Fat: 4 g
- Protein: 87 g

Baked Potatoes with Bacon

Preparation Time: 5 minutes

Cooking Time: 27/30 minutes

Servings: 4

Ingredients:

- 4 potatoes, scrubbed, halved, cut lengthwise
- 1 tbsp olive oil
- Salt and black pepper to taste (very little)
- 4 oz bacon, chopped

Directions:

1. Preheat the air fryer to 390°F.
2. Season the potatoes with olive oil salt and pepper. Place them in the greased basket, cut side down.
3. Cook for 15 minutes, turn, add bacon and cook for 12-15 minutes or until potatoes are golden brown and bacon is crispy.
4. Serve.

Nutrition:

- Calories: 150
- Carbohydrates: 9 g
- Fat: 7 g
- Protein: 62 g

Classic French Fries

Preparation Time: 5 minutes

Cooking Time: 20/22 minutes

Servings: 2

Ingredients:

- 2 russet potatoes, cut into strips
- 2 tbsp olive oil
- Kosher salt and black pepper to taste (very little)
- 1/2 cup garlic aioli
- Cooking Spray

Directions:

1. Preheat the fryer to 400°F.
2. Spray the fryer basket with cooking spray.
3. In a bowl, season potato strips with olive oil, salt and black pepper. Place in the fryer and cook for 20-22 minutes, turning once halfway through cooking, until crispy.
4. Serve with garlic aioli.

Nutrition:

- Calories: 120
- Carbohydrates: 7 g
- Fat: 4 g
- Protein: 56 g

Honey Roasted Carrots

Preparation Time: 5 minutes
Cooking Time: 12 minutes
Servings: 4
Ingredients:

- 1 Tablespoon Honey, Raw
- 2 Cups Baby Carrots
- 1 Tablespoon Olive Oil
- Sea Salt & Black Pepper to Taste (very little)

Directions:

1. Put the baby carrots, honey, olive oil, salt and pepper in a bowl, and mix well so the carrots are well seasoned.
2. Bake at 390F for 12 minutes and serve.

Nutrition:

- Calories: 82
- Protein: 61 g
- Fat: 3.2 g
- Carbohydrates: 2.1 g

Chapter 9: Dessert Recipes

Cheesecake with Ricotta

Preparation Time: 15 minutes

Cooking Time: 25 minutes

Servings: 8

Ingredients:

- 17.6 oz. Ricotta cheese
- 3 eggs
- ¾ cup sugar
- 3 tablespoons corn starch
- 1 tablespoon fresh lemon juice
- 2 teaspoons vanilla extract
- 1 teaspoon fresh lemon zest, finely grated

Directions:

1. Preheat the air fryer to 320°F.
2. In a large bowl, place ricotta cheese, eggs, sugar, cornstarch, vanilla, lemon zest and juice and mix until well combined.
3. Place mixture in a pan suitable for the air fryer.

4. Place the pan in the basket of the air fryer and bake for 25 minutes at 320°F.
5. Place the cake pan onto a wire rack to cool completely.
6. Refrigerate overnight before serving.

Nutrition:

- Calories: 97
- Fat: 6.6 g
- Carbohydrates: 15.7 g
- Protein: 92.2 g

Berry Crumble with Lemon

Preparation Time: 30 minutes

Cooking Time: 20 min

Servings: 6

Ingredients:

- 12 oz fresh strawberries
- 7 oz fresh raspberries
- 5 oz fresh blueberries
- 5 tbsp cold margarine
- 2 tbsp lemon juice
- 1 cup flour
- 1/2 cup sugar
- 1 tbsp water
- A pinch of salt (very little)

Directions:

1. Gently massage and chop berries, but make sure chunks remain.
2. Mix the berries with the lemon juice and 2 tablespoons of sugar.
3. Place berry mixture in the bottom of a prepared round cake.
4. In a bowl, mix the flour with the salt and sugar.

5. Add the water and rub in the margarine with your fingers until the mixture becomes crumbly.
6. Roll out the resulting dough and form it into a disk the width of your cake Pan or base.
7. Lay the crispy dough disk on top of the berries.
8. Bake in the deep fryer at 390°F for 20 minutes.

Nutrition:

- Calories: 250
- Protein: 89.2 g
- Fat: 10.28 g
- Carbohydrates: 38.09 g

Apple Treat with Raisins

Preparation Time: 15 minutes

Cooking Time: 10 min

Servings: 4

Ingredients:

- 4 apples, cored
- 1 1/2 oz almonds
- ¾ oz raisins
- 2 tbsp sugar
- Powdered sugar, to taste

Directions:

1. Preheat air fryer to 360°F
2. In a bowl, mix sugar, almonds, raisins well.
3. Blend the mixture with a hand mixer.
4. Fill cored apples with almond mixture.
5. Place the prepared apples in the basket of the air fryer and bake for 10 minutes at 360°F. Serve with powdered sugar.

Nutrition:

- Calories: 188
- Protein: 72.88 g
- Fat: 5.64 g
- Carbohydrates: 35.63 g

French Toast Bites

Preparation Time: 5 minutes

Cooking Time: 15 minutes

Servings: 8

Ingredients:

- 1 cup Almond milk
- 1 tbsp. Cinnamon
- 2 tbsp. Sweetener
- 3 eggs
- 4 pieces wheat bread

Directions:

1. Preheat the fryer to 360°F.
2. In a bowl, beat the eggs and dilute with the almond milk.
3. In another bowl mix 1/3 cup sweetener with plenty of cinnamon.
4. Cut the bread in half, knead the pieces and press together to form bread balls
5. Dip the bread balls in the egg and then roll in the cinnamon sugar, making sure to coat completely.
6. Place the coated bread balls in the air fryer and bake for 15 minutes at 360°F.

Nutrition:

- Calories: 189
- Protein: 49 g
- Fat: 11 g
- Carbohydrates: 17 g

Cinnamon Sugar Roasted Chickpeas

Preparation Time: 5 minutes
Cooking Time: 10 minutes
Servings: 2
Ingredients:

- 1 tbsp. sweetener
- 1 tbsp. cinnamon
- 1 C. chickpeas

Directions:

1. Preheat the fryer to 390°.
2. Rinse and drain chickpeas.
3. In a bowl place drained chickpeas along with cinnamon, sweetener and mix everything to season the chickpeas well and then place in the air fryer.
4. Set the temperature to 390°F and set the time to 10 minutes.
5. Serve and enjoy

Nutrition:

- Calories: 111
- Protein: 46 g
- Fat: 19 g
- Carbohydrates: 18 g

Conclusion

Inside this book you have found a series of recipes divided by meal type for people coming out of Bariatric surgery to prepare with the Air Fryer.

Those who have undergone bariatric surgery are aware that in the post-operative rehabilitation phase it is essential to follow without error a specific diet directed to the intake of light foods, first of all liquid, semi-liquid and normal, with very low fat and salt content and rich in protein and fiber.

With the recipes you will find in this book you can cook many light and tasty dishes with the help of the air fryer that as we know allows you to cook with very little added fat any type of food, maintaining a flavor and a crispness very close to the classic frying but at the same time with a lightness suitable for those who must control the intake of fat.

We hope our book can be an extra help for all those who must follow a post bariatric diet without living the same diet as a nightmare.